YOU CAN'T POSSIBLY COLOR THIS!

AN IMPOSSIBLE OPTICAL ILLUSION ACTIVITY BOOK

GIANNI A. SARCONE

MoonDance

Brimming with creative inspiration, how-to projects, and
information to enrich your everyday life, Quarto Knows is
destination for those pursuing their interests and passion
site and dig deeper with our books into your area of inte
Quarto Creates, Quarto Cooks, Quarto Homes, Quarto L

© 2017 Quarto Publishing Group USA Inc.
Text & Illustrations © 2017 Gianni A. Sarcone

First Published in 2017 by MoonDance Press, an imprint of The Quarto Group.
6 Orchard Road, Suite 100, Lake Forest, CA 92630, USA.
T (949) 380-7510 F (949) 380-7575 **www.QuartoKnows.com**

MoonDance Press titles are also available at discount for retail, wholesale,
promotional, and bulk purchase. For details, contact the Special Sales Manager by
email at specialsales@quarto.com or by mail at The Quarto Group, Attn: Special Sales
Manager, 401 Second Avenue North, Suite 310, Minneapolis, MN 55401 USA.

ISBN: 978-1-63322-351-6

Design and cover by Melissa Gerber
Layout by Elliot Kreloff

Printed in China
10 9 8 7 6 5 4 3 2 1

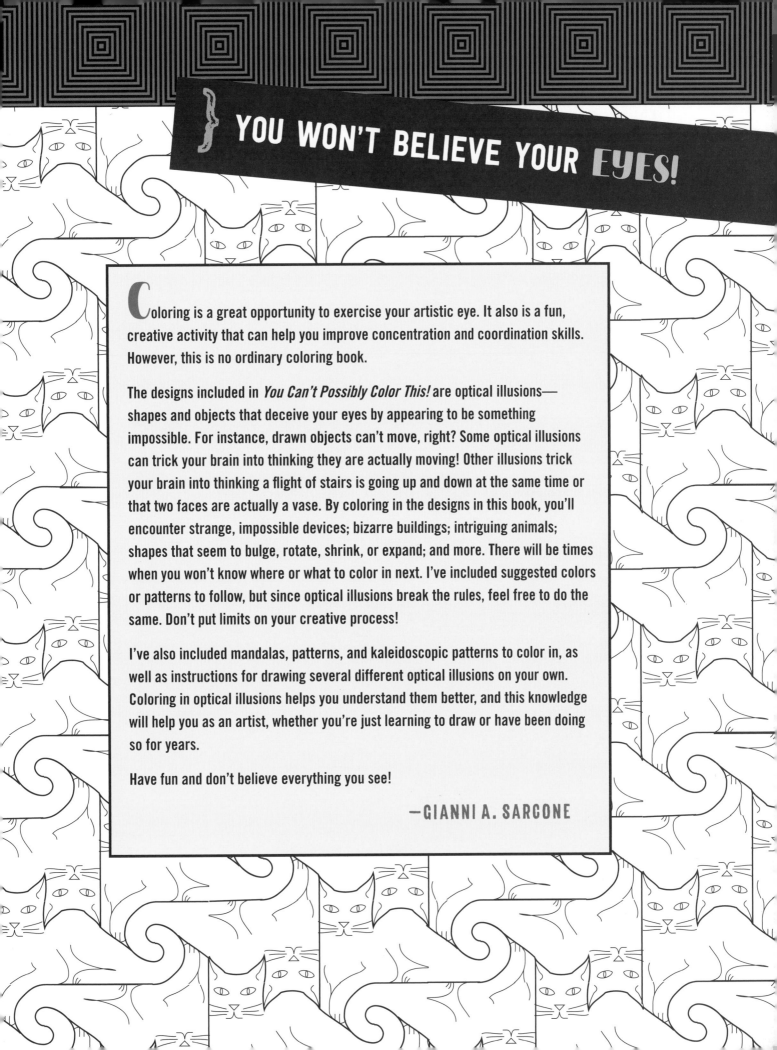

YOU WON'T BELIEVE YOUR EYES!

Coloring is a great opportunity to exercise your artistic eye. It also is a fun, creative activity that can help you improve concentration and coordination skills. However, this is no ordinary coloring book.

The designs included in *You Can't Possibly Color This!* are optical illusions—shapes and objects that deceive your eyes by appearing to be something impossible. For instance, drawn objects can't move, right? Some optical illusions can trick your brain into thinking they are actually moving! Other illusions trick your brain into thinking a flight of stairs is going up and down at the same time or that two faces are actually a vase. By coloring in the designs in this book, you'll encounter strange, impossible devices; bizarre buildings; intriguing animals; shapes that seem to bulge, rotate, shrink, or expand; and more. There will be times when you won't know where or what to color in next. I've included suggested colors or patterns to follow, but since optical illusions break the rules, feel free to do the same. Don't put limits on your creative process!

I've also included mandalas, patterns, and kaleidoscopic patterns to color in, as well as instructions for drawing several different optical illusions on your own. Coloring in optical illusions helps you understand them better, and this knowledge will help you as an artist, whether you're just learning to draw or have been doing so for years.

Have fun and don't believe everything you see!

—GIANNI A. SARCONE

This intricate Islamic decoration is built on a combination of repeating squares and hexagons.

This pattern features intersecting *quatrefoils*. A quatrefoil is a decorative framework that includes a symmetrical shape of four partially overlapping circles.

SHAPES THAT MOVE

If you color this pattern properly, the black triangles on the left side will appear to be moving up while the ones on the right will seem to be moving down. This is known as an *autokinetic* effect.

Fill the blank triangles with shades of gray. Their bases should be darker than their tips.

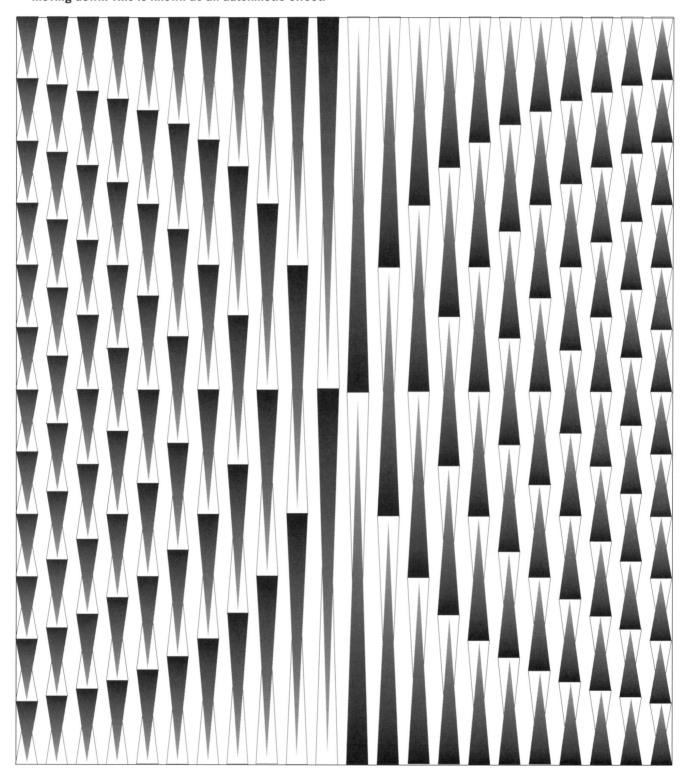

If you color this pattern properly, the circular drops may start to move up and down slightly.

Don't color the white crescent shapes at the base of the circles.

DRAW FUNNY, IMPOSSIBLE WIENER DOGS IN 6 STEPS!

1 **2**

3 **4**

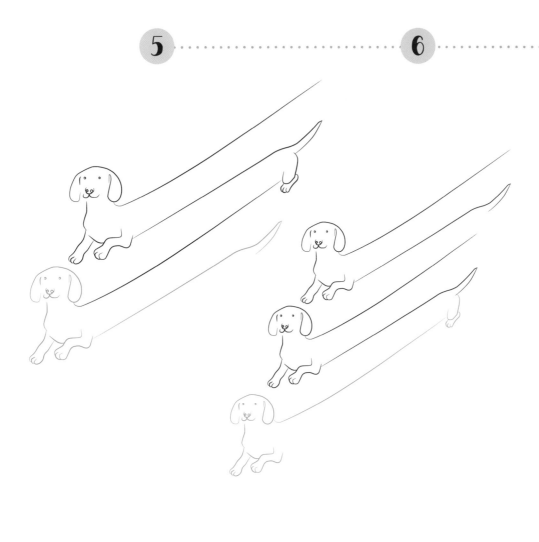

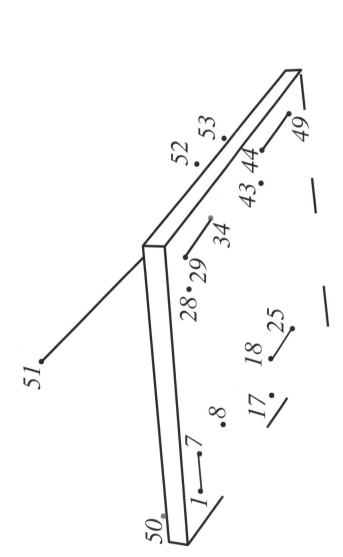

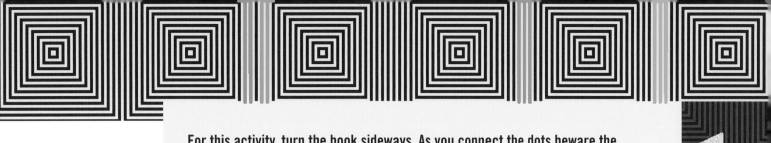

For this activity, turn the book sideways. As you connect the dots beware the red dots. That's where things get tricky and impossible! Then, try coloring in the whole picture. Can it be done?

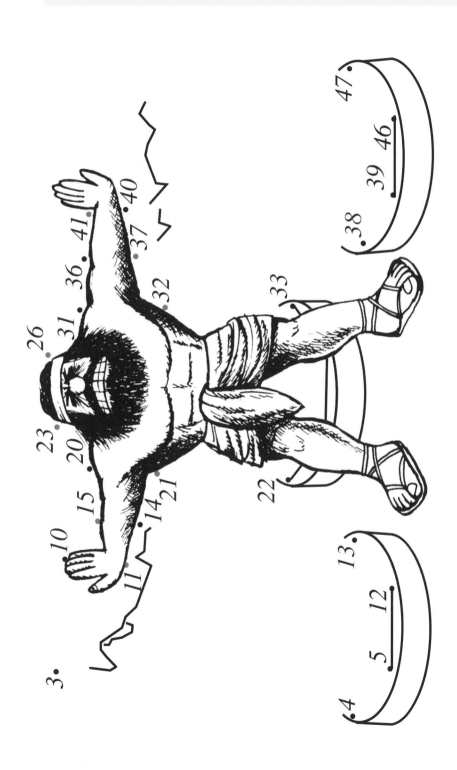

Take a close look at Lea's bizarre house. Does the window open inward or outward? Is the front door narrow or wide? There are no correct answers to these questions because these are impossible objects that can't exist in our 3-dimensional world!

Do all the beams of this structure meet at right angles? Notice how parts of this appear to come toward you and away from you at the same time.

Geometric elements featured in this pattern. 1 2

 Mayan Calendar Wheel

DRAW MAGIC SPHERES

1 With an erasable pencil, draw parallel diagonal lines across the opposite page.

2 Draw circles over the diagonal lines, and then erase the lines inside the circles.

3 Connect the broken lines with curved lines.

4 Add color!

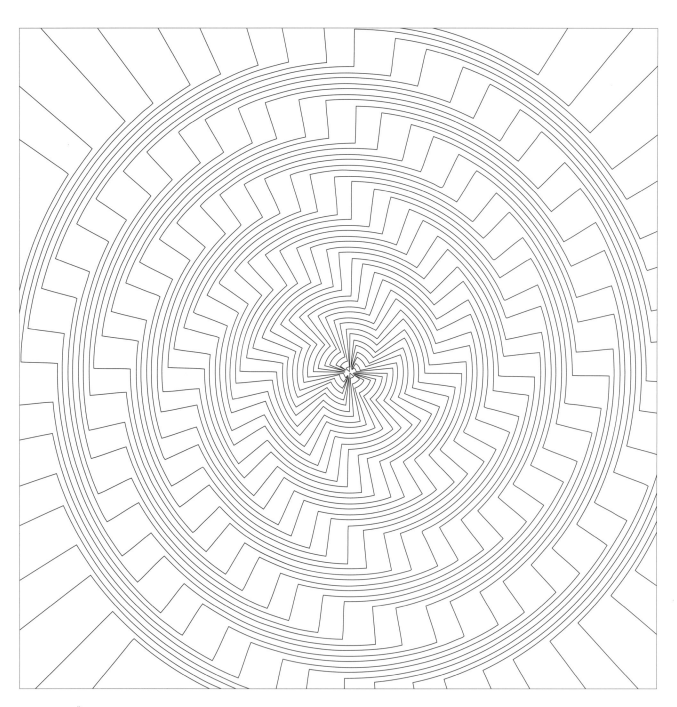

Color the patterns using this color sequence. The image will appear to shrink.

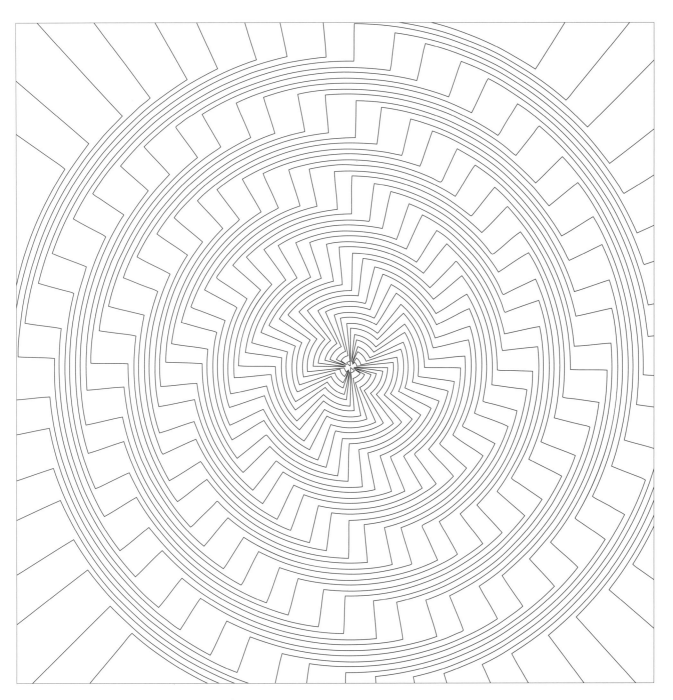

Try it again using different colors.

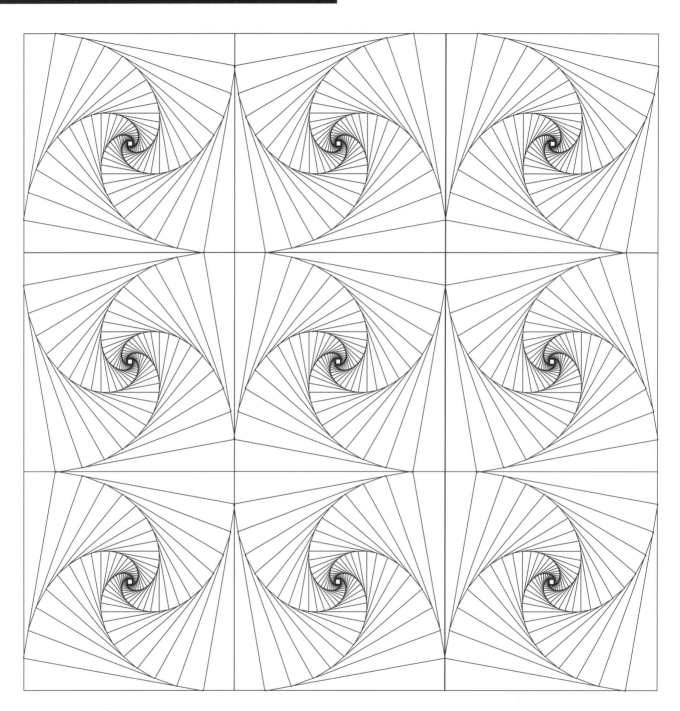

Color the patterns using this color sequence. The image will appear to expand.

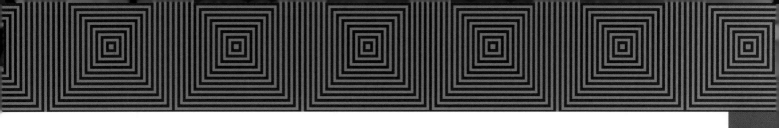

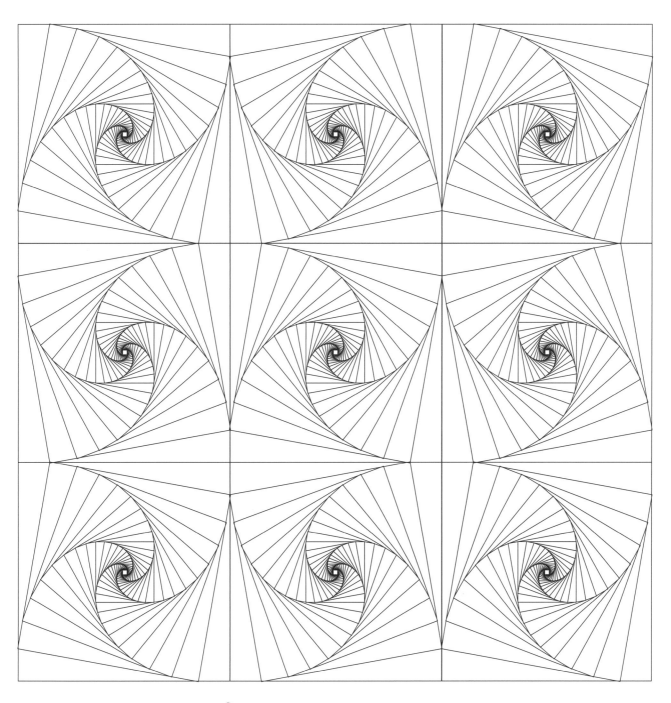

Try it again using different colors.

The ancient Greeks created single-path labyrinths called *Cretans*. These types of "mazes" only have one path to the center of the puzzle. They are built around a base, or heart, that looks sort of like a cross (see figure 1). Follow the examples below to draw your own labyrinths.

Figure 1

The heart of the Cretan labyrinth

Figure 2

Figure 3

You can draw amazing labyrinths or Celtic patterns with what are called C-scrolls and S-scrolls. Practice the scrolls below and then try creating a design like the one you'll see when you turn the page. Finally, color in the design!

A spiral labyrinth made with C- and S-scrolls.

C-scroll

S-scroll

C- and S-scrolls combined

Try drawing this with thicker lines.

Add more detail!

Try it with disjointed lines.

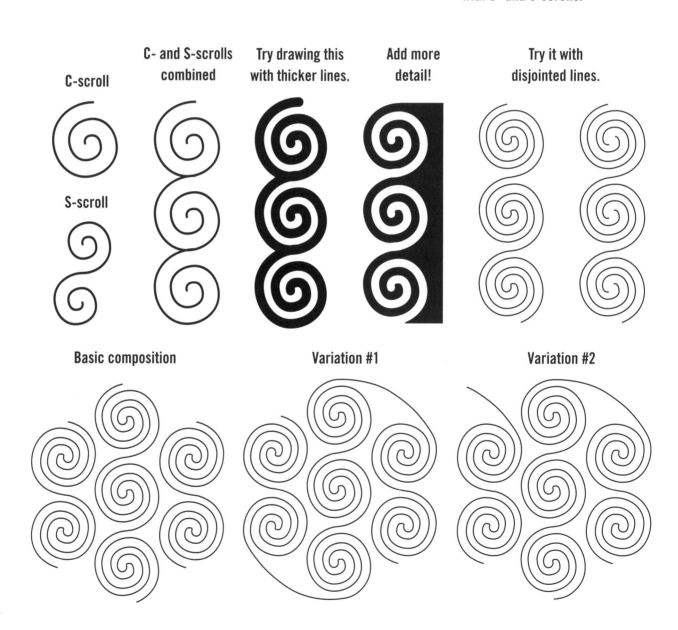

Basic composition

Variation #1

Variation #2

PSYCHEDELIC MANDALAS

Mandalas are geometric patterns that start at a central dot and work outward in repetitive patterns.
Color these in as you see fit!

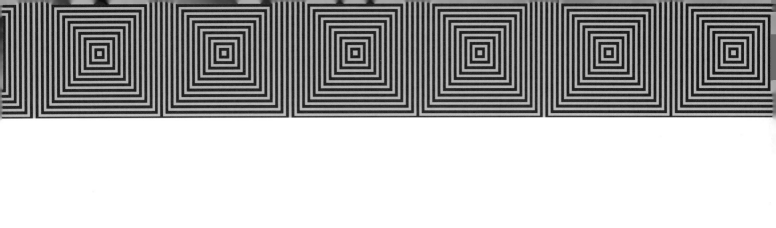

Color in the 3-D cubes.

All you need to do in order to make these objects look like they're floating above the table is to draw their shadows as shown below.

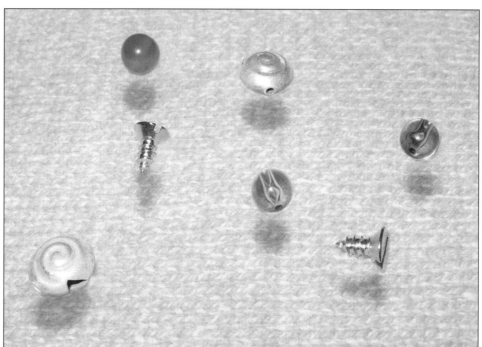

When you place a clear glass or bottle filled with water in front of a lined background, the lines inside the glass become distorted. This is called *refraction*. Try to color the lines and glasses.

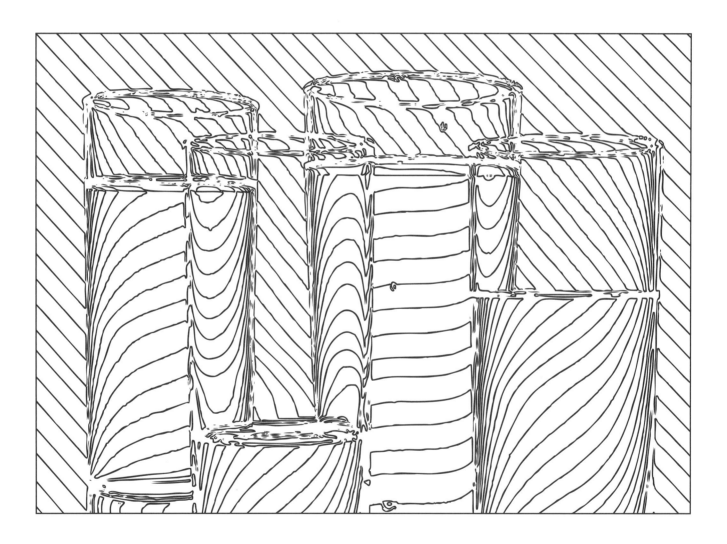

} TSP ART

Check out the image of the Mona Lisa on the opposite page. This version of the famous painting by Leonardo da Vinci was created by Craig S. Kaplan, an assistant professor of computer science at the University of Waterloo in Ontario, Canada. He studies the interactions between computer graphics, art, and mathematics. The image here was created by a computer and is called TSP Art. It is a single, non-intersecting line that wiggles and bends to cover the canvas.

Choose whatever colors you wish to fill in the Mona Lisa. Use the example below as a guide.

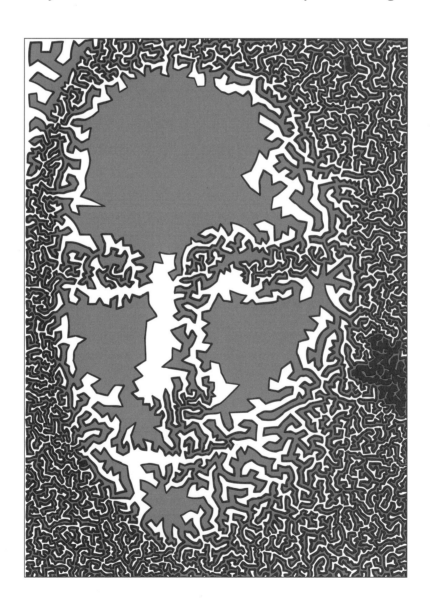

Some patterns are called *recursive* when they contain shapes or items that repeat themselves continuously. Here are recursive elephants walking along a spiral. Can you color them in?

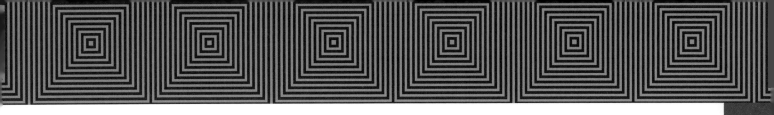

Draw your own recursive pattern here.

The Droste effect is when an image contains a smaller version of itself, which then contains an even smaller version… and so on. This gives the illusion that it goes on forever.

To create your own Droste effect, you will need the use of a photocopier.

1 Using an erasable pencil, draw an oval shape for the head. Make sure you leave room on the page for the rest of the image. Draw two lines as shown.

2 Use the dividing lines as a guide to draw half of the face.

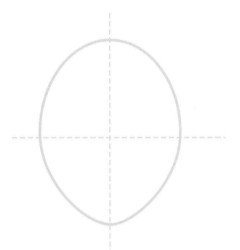

3 Draw the other half of the face.

4 Draw the cup.

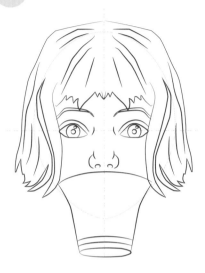

5 Draw the torso along with the arms.

6 Complete the drawing by adding the details of the lower part of the body.

7 Once you're happy with your drawing, trace over the lines with a pen. Erase the pencil lines.

8 Now for the fun part. Place your final drawing on the photocopier and reduce to 13% of the original size. Cut out the tiny girl.

9 Photocopy the new, little girl at a reduced size and cut her out. How long can you keep doing this before there's nothing left to see!

10 Once you're done, glue the biggest photocopy on top of the saucer of your original drawing. Then glue the other photocopies as shown. Photocopy the final collage and color it in.

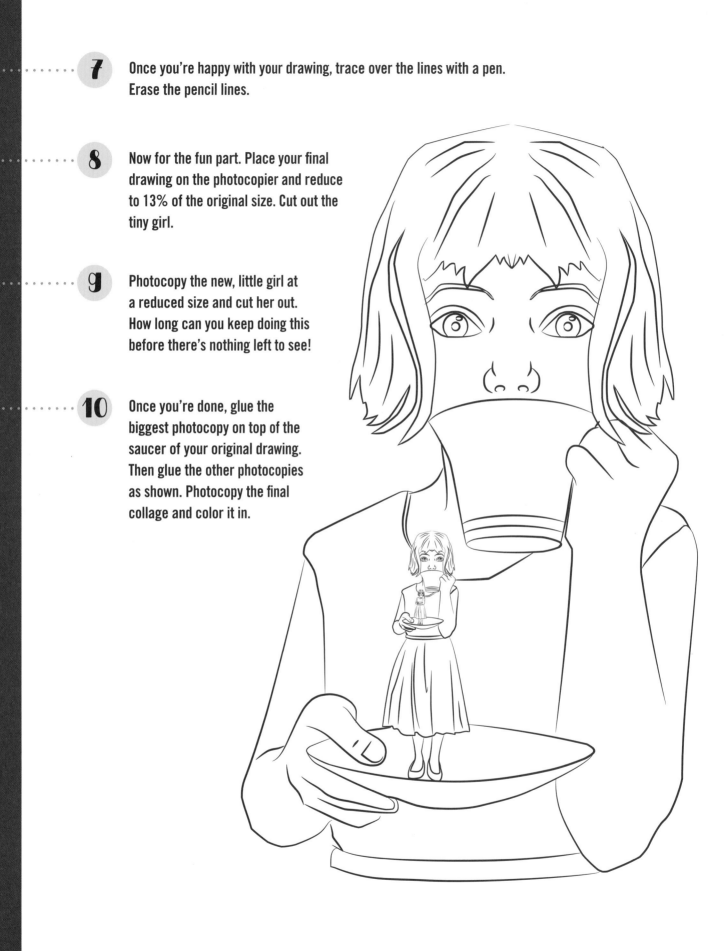

Color in the drawings on the next two pages, using these two examples to inspire you.

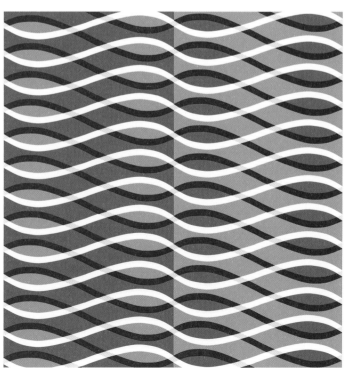

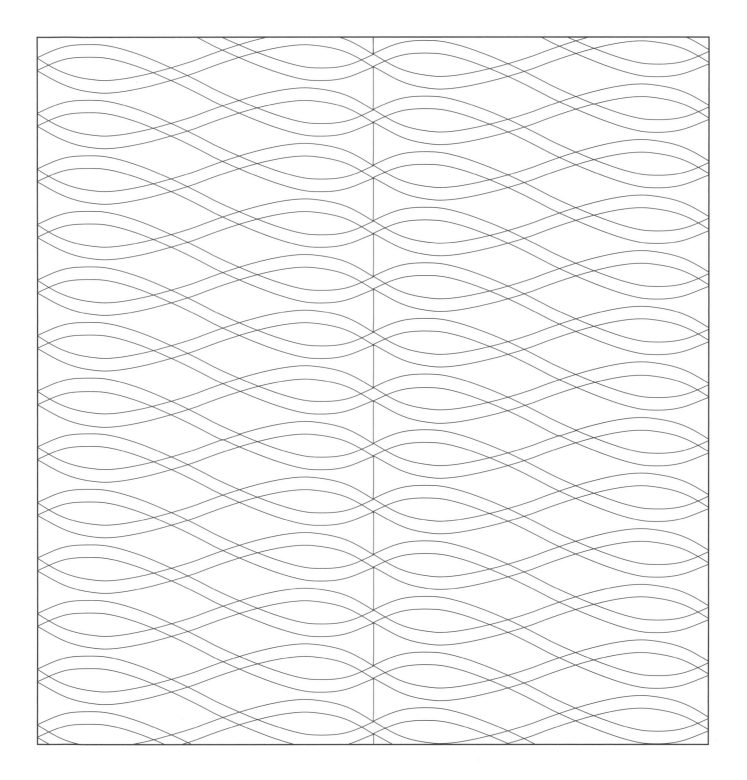

SQUARES IN SQUARES IN SQUARES

Use vivid colors to color this in!

Is this staircase going up or down? Good question!
Color it in and then turn the page to create your own impossible staircase.

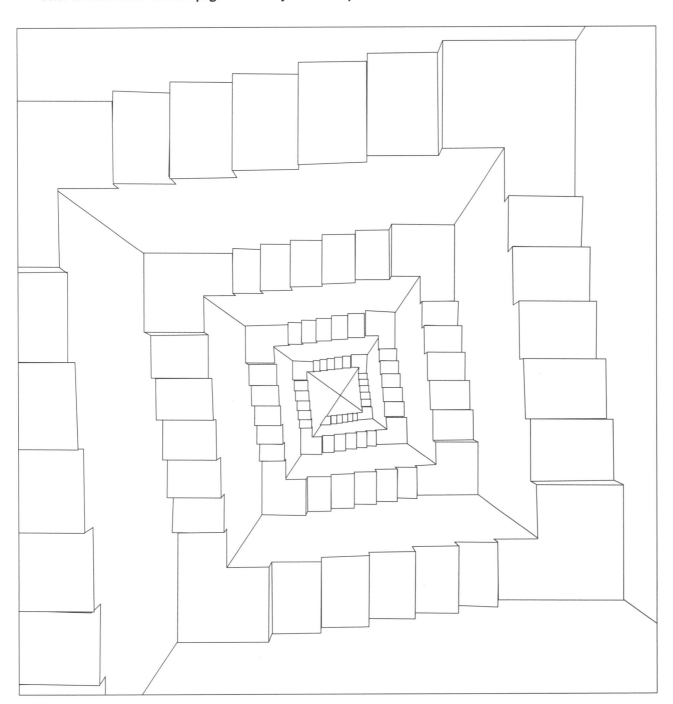

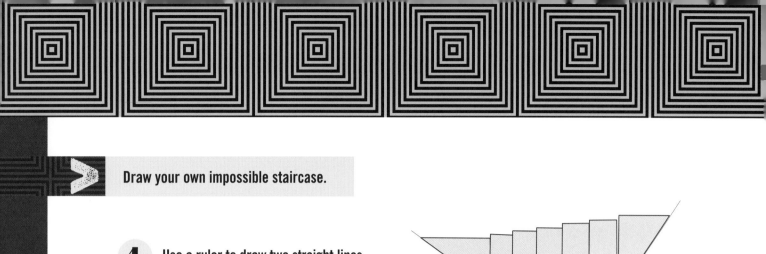

Draw your own impossible staircase.

1 Use a ruler to draw two straight lines intersecting at right angles. Draw a set of stairs between the two lines.

2 Continue drawing stairs as you move around the two lines. Make sure the stairs get smaller as you head "down."

3 When you think you have enough stairs, color the four walls of the stairwell with a neutral shade. Make sure the bottom of the stairwell is darker than the top.

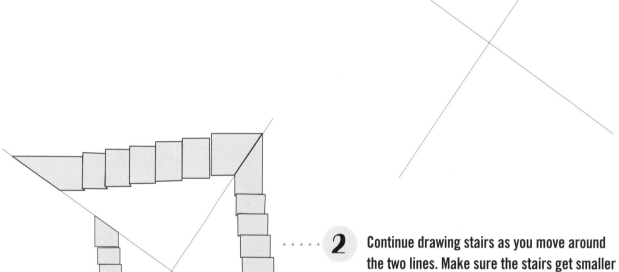

NEVER-ENDING PATTERN

This is a *fractal* tree. That means it was created using the same pattern over and over again. Color this one in and then try drawing one on the opposite page.

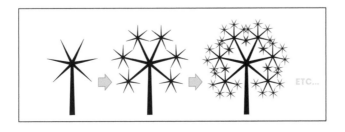

SINGLE LINE DRAWINGS

Can you draw the following animals without taking your pencil off the paper? This is called a *unicursal drawing,* and the rules are that you can't lift your pencil as you draw and you can't retrace any line.

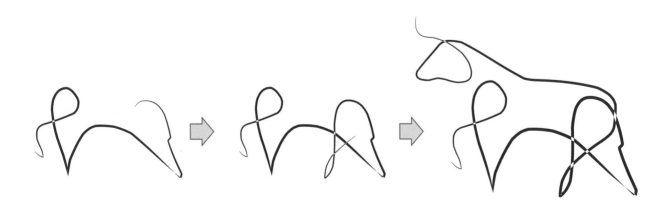

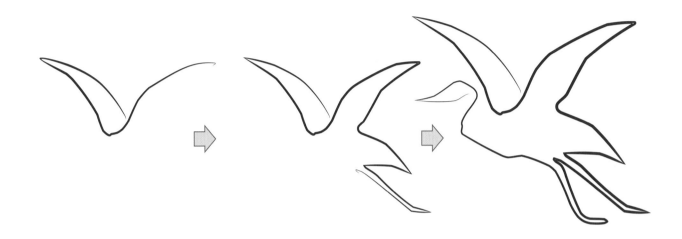

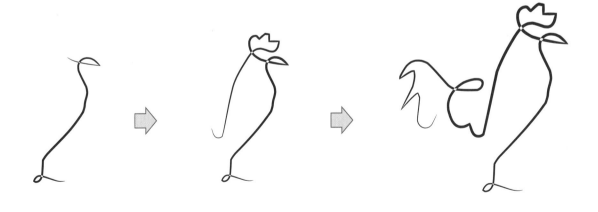

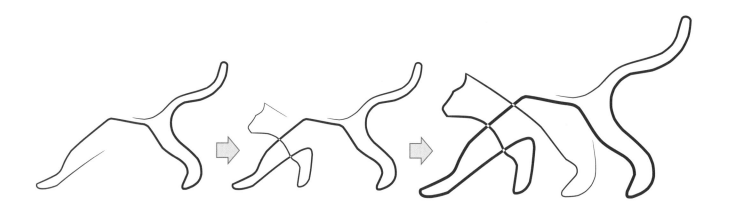

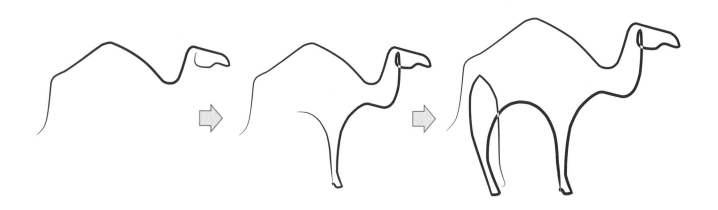

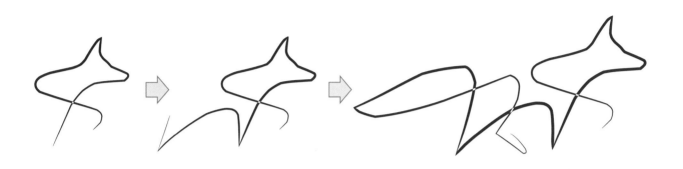

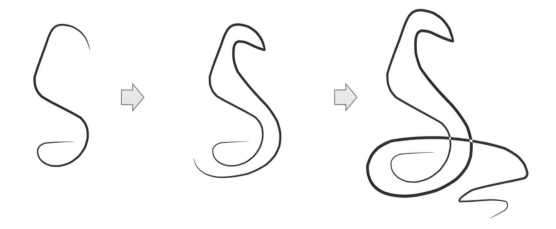

If you color this series of circular patterns correctly, they will appear to move and expand. For best results, leave one out of every four spaces blank.

For best results, leave one out of every four spaces blank.

1. Cut out the women on the next pages.

2. Then cut out the clothing as shown here.

3. Hold the cut-outs up against any background for an original design.

4. Take photographs of your favorites.

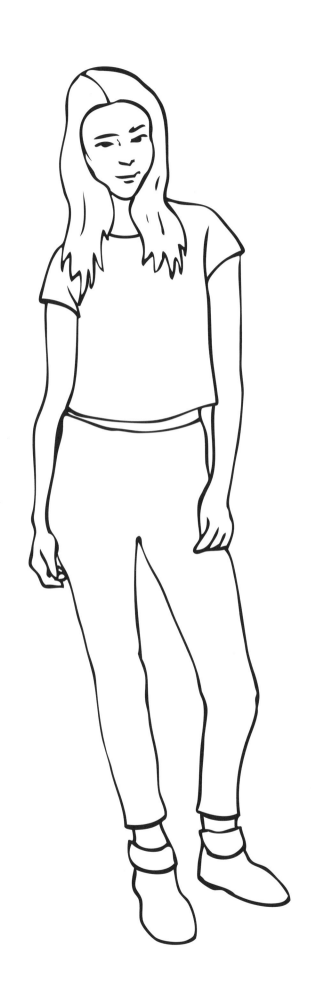

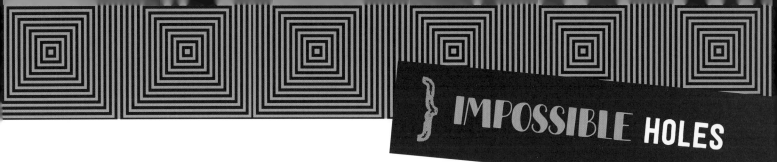
Can you color this in so that it makes sense to your eyes?

THE VASE ILLUSION

Follow the step-by-step illustrations to draw this illusion in which the shape of a glass gets confused with the children's faces.

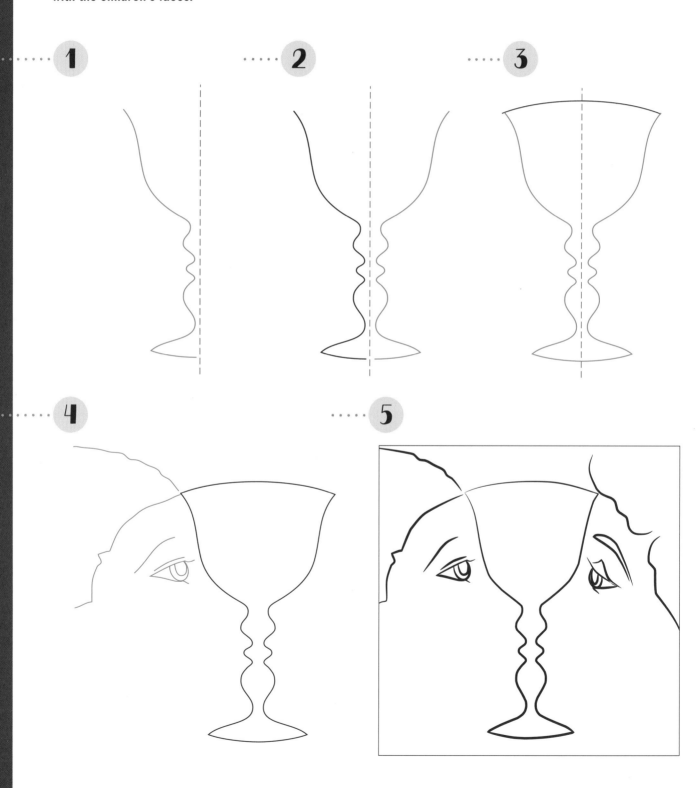

Color this in and then turn the page to make your own.

Follow the step-by-step illustrations on this page to make your own 3-D teardrop pattern.

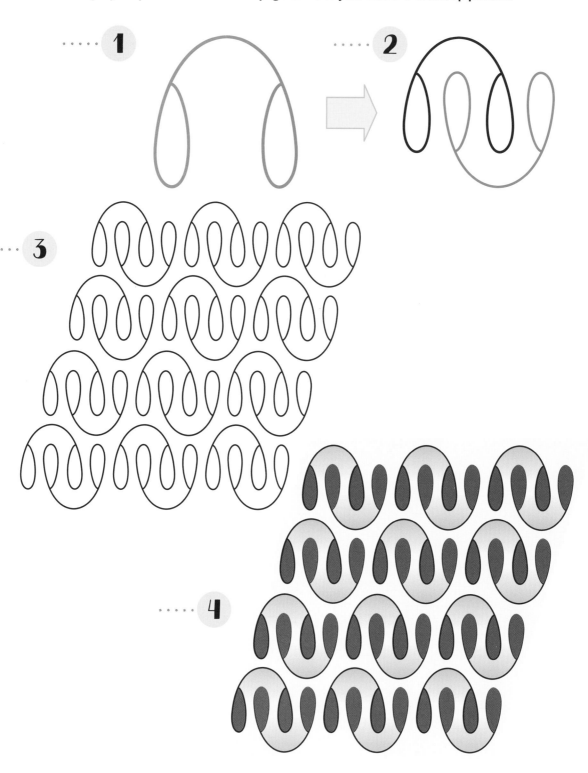

Can you color this in? You might need to try it a couple of times!

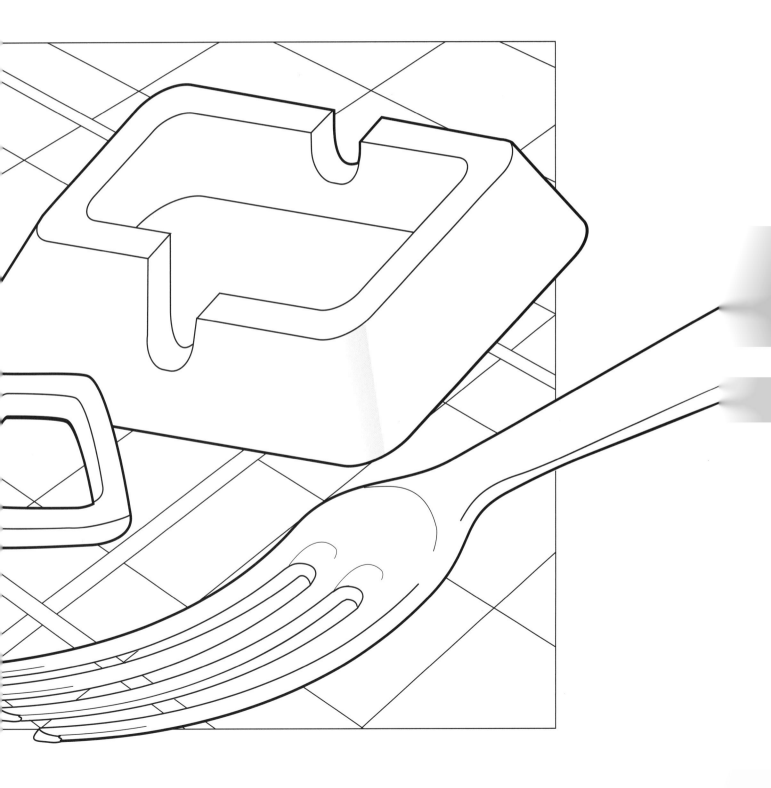

BULGING ILLUSION

Use contrasting colors to fill in this bulging illusion.

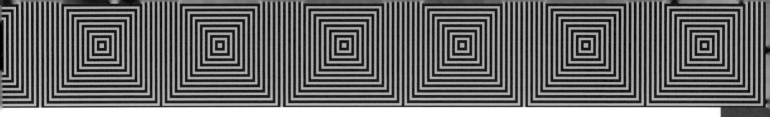

1

2

3

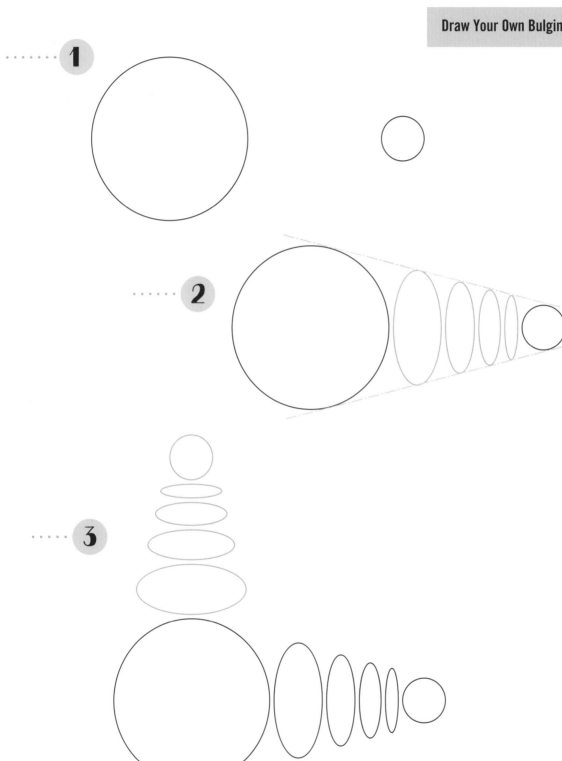

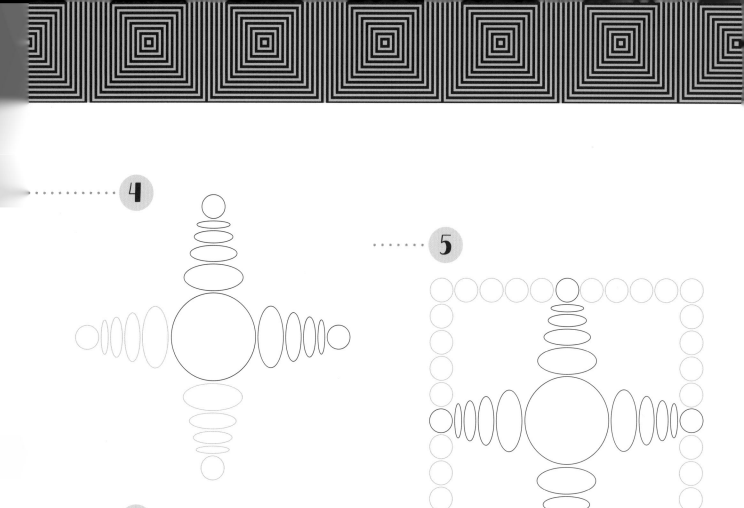

4

5

6

7

This illusion seems to pulse outward. Can you recreate this effect?
Color in the pattern on the opposite page using this page as a guide.

This illusion seems to shrink. See if you can recreate this effect using this page as a guide.

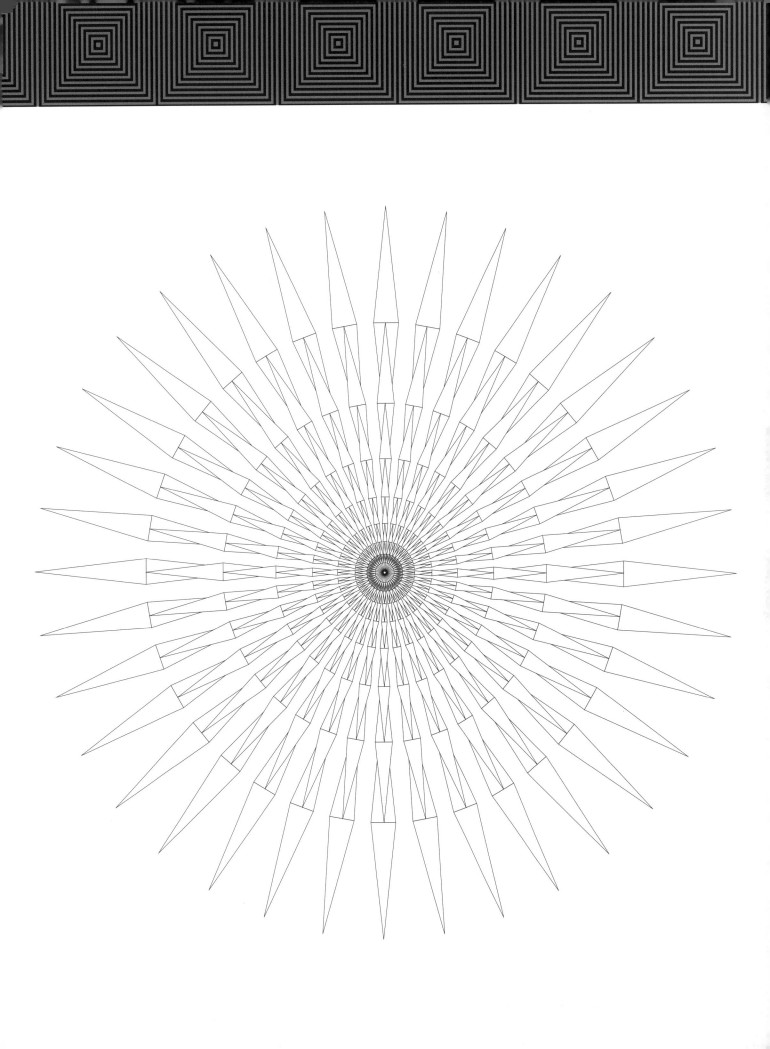

Each of the illusions on this page start with the same simple spiral. Use the following graph pages to attempt these impossible rolled sheets. Can you come up with any of your own?

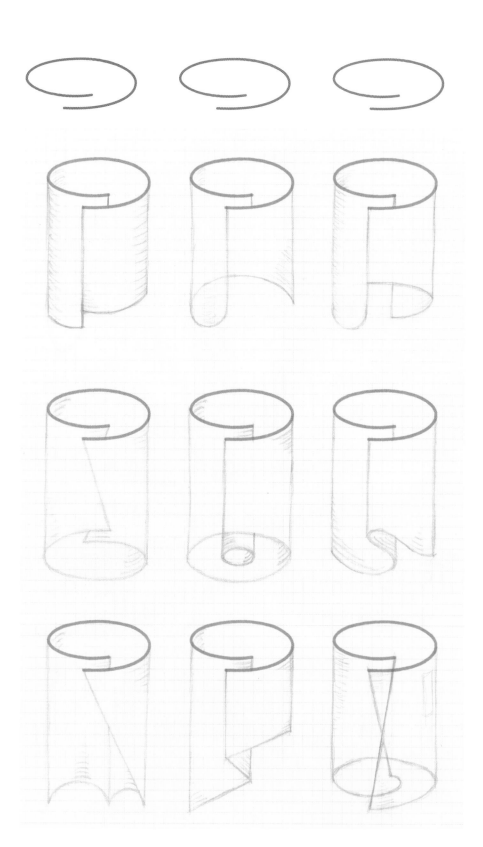

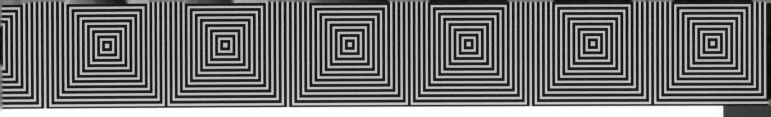

THAT'S IMPOSSIBLE!

Figures 1 and 2 can be placed together to form a cool optical illusion (figure 3).
Try drawing this weird illusion on the opposite page. Then, color in the following page.

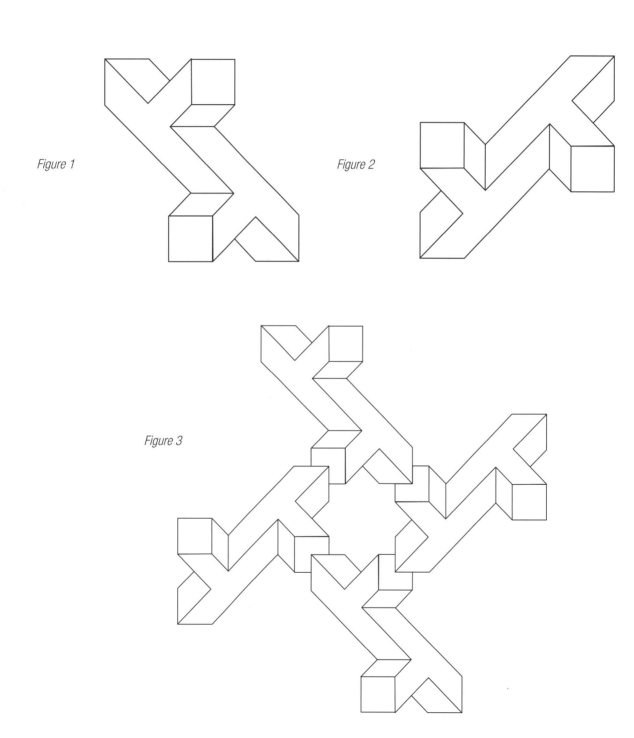

Figure 1

Figure 2

Figure 3

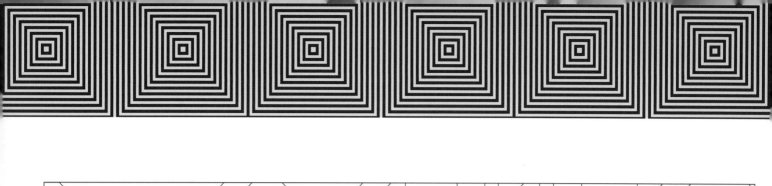

Use these expanding and shrinking illusions as inspiration to color in the drawings on the next pages.